Edinburgh in old picture postcards the Old Town

by
Donald Lindgren

European Library – Zaltbommel/Netherlands

I wish to record my thanks to all of those who helped me with information, photographs and postcards during my research for this first volume of a city that I have come to love as my home. My special thanks are given to Margaret K. Graham, who so graciously allowed me to use many postcards from her extensive collection. I am thankful to my good friend Alex Harkes, who has always encouraged me and made valuable suggestions as he has proof-read and corrected my text. Any errors are my own and I accept full responsibility for them.

Books by the same author:
Designs for Christian Living
Musselburgh in old picture postcards volumes 1 and 2
The Firth of Forth in old picture postcards volumes 1 and 2
The Work of Reginald P. Phillimore in old picture postcards

About this book:
This first volume of Edinburgh is one of a planned series, by the same author, on the capital city of Scotland. I have tried to confine my photographs, postcards and text for this first volume in the series to the Old Town, although I have 'strayed' a little, and included a few important places that are outside that area. The next volume, which is presently in preparation, will be published in the near future and will include Leith, Newhaven and the New Town.

GB ISBN 90 288 5865 2 / CIP

© 1994 European Library – Zaltbommel/Netherlands

INTRODUCTION

My love affair with the beautiful city of Edinburgh began 32 years ago when I arrived by train at Waverley Railway Station late one autumn evening to begin my post graduate studies at Edinburgh University. After a taxi ride through a thick fog, referred to at that time as a 'dirty night', I arrived at St. Leonard's Hall, the former home of James Nelson, the famous Edinburgh publisher, where arriving foreign students were temporarily housed by the University until they found 'digs' with local landlords. I was welcomed to Edinburgh by a kind lady who gave me a cup of tea and showed me to my room. The next morning when I opened the curtains and saw, for the first time, a view of Salisbury Crags and Arthur's Seat with sheep grazing on the sloping hills, I could not believe that I was in the middle of the Capital of Scotland. I thought I was dreaming. From that first dramatic introduction to the city, that has become my beloved home since I was a university student, I have loved Edinburgh and believe it to be one of the most beautiful cities in the world. This is truly a city that is set on a hill, in fact three hills, and it never ceases to bring to me wonder and amazement at such dignified beauty and grandeur. The postcards in this book, mostly from scenes in the Old Town, show us what Edinburgh used to look like between 1890 and 1930, but the city is, in so many ways, ageless and although in some parts there are great changes, the great historical buildings of the Old Town are very much as they were, except that cars and buses pass by them today instead of the trams and horse-drawn carriages of yesterday.

The city is one of dramatic extremes and its powerful influence upon its people is greater than in most cities. It had such an influence on its famous son, Robert Louis Stevenson, who had a life-long love-hate affair with his birthplace. Stevenson loved his home city but he suffered more than most from the cold and damp and sometimes inhospitable weather. The east wind was called Edinburgh's great enemy; the channel, or hollow, between the Old Town and the New, 'A Cave of winds'. Its two most famous literary sons, Stevenson and Sir Walter Scott, will always be associated with Edinburgh.

The Old Town received the nickname 'Auld Reekie' (Old Smoky) last century because of the volume of smoke emitted from the coal burning fires in the homes of its citizens. The steam trains of the North British and Caledonian Railways also added to the plume of smoke that hung heavily over the city. Today all of that has changed and the name, although still used with affection, no longer applies. Another nickname, 'The Athens of the North' certainly does apply, not only because Edinburgh is a site of culture, learning, literature and science, but also because visitors come from all over the world and discover in its topography, architecture and its classical beauty a resemblance to the Greek Capital.

Its history is ancient. Its origin is obscure and clouded because its early records were almost destroyed by Edward I during his invasion of the city and what was left was completely destroyed when Oliver Cromwell took up residence in the Castle after his victory over the Scots at Dunbar. We know that in pre-Christian times the lands around the city and Castle Rock were occupied by the Picts. From our knowledge of the customs and habits of the Picts through the excavation of their buildings and homes, in Orkney and the North of Scotland, it is reasonable to suggest that they built upon the Castle Rock. In 58 AD, however, they were driven out of the Lothians by the Romans. Only a few miles from Edinburgh, in Musselburgh on Inveresk Hill, the Romans built a large fortress. Only recently, while preparing new burial ground in the cemetery, on that same hill, part of the foundation of this extensive fortress was unearthed and studied by archaeologists from the University and Museum. I was invited by the East Lothian District Council to consecrate the new burial ground that is only a few feet away from that ancient Roman fortress where the Romans lived and died and were undoubtedly buried. When the Romans finally left Scotland the Saxons advanced and possessed the lowlands from the River Tweed to the Firth of Forth and added it to their Kingdom of Northumbria. Around 617 AD Edwin of Deira fortified Castle Rock and gave his name both to the Castle and the Burgh. These Northumbrian Saxons held the area until 956 when it became part of Scotland.

It was Malcolm Canmore, whose Palace was first at Dunfermline, who made Edinburgh his capital. It was in Edinburgh that the first national parliament was held and united the Saxons and Normans with the Scots to make a people of strength and character prepared to build a great nation. Malcolm's saintly wife, Margaret, also made her profound influence for good upon the new nation. Her piety, devotion, and good works were legend and so sincere that she was eventually made a saint by the Roman Catholic Church; the only Scot to have been so honoured. The oldest part of Edinburgh Castle is, appropriately, named St. Margaret's Chapel.

The heart and soul of the Old Town was the noble thoroughfare named simply the High Street but later 'dignified' to the grand title of 'The Royal Mile'. For centuries life was concentrated in this backbone of the city with its ribs, called closes and wynds, branching out on both sides. This small area, confined by the valley of the Nor' Loch, had more houses and people, and perhaps witnessed more historical events of national importance, than any similar place in Europe. Many of the tenements, or 'lands' as they are called in Old Edinburgh, were impressive as they rose 16 storeys high and could be seen towering above the crown of St. Giles' Cathedral. These 'lands' were the world's first skyscrapers hundreds of years before that term was used to describe the buildings built in New York City this century. This noble street, stretching from the Castle to Holyrood Palace, still holds many secrets of life and death in Old Edinburgh. It evokes the wonder and admiration of its visitors and the pride of its citizens. During the International Festival, held each year, the High Street comes alive with street theatre and strollers admiring the charm of this distinctive part of the capital city.

Not only was the Castle the fortification and defence of the Old Town but also the High Street, with its limited access. On the north side of this 'canyon' made of buildings no exit could be found by the passenger carrying carriages until Leith Wynd, near North Bridge, was reached. Only in favourable weather could the sedan chairs exit by a short cut into the valley of the dried out Nor' Loch at Halkerston's Wynd, named after David Halkerston, who held out bravely, to his death, against the English invader, The Earl of Hertford, when he made his onslaught against the capital.

It was the craving for more light, air and space that a landmark decision was made that resulted in the building of the North Bridge. In 1772 the way was finally opened and passable between the High Street and the fields to the north that became the New Town. The society of the upper strata of the Old Town began to flow north to build their spacious homes there and the High Street was left to the more humble residents. So important was the North Bridge that Lord Rosebery called it 'The foundation of the City's beauty'. Now, as you read the text and view the pictures, I hope that you will discover something of the majesty and wonder of the Old Town; the ancient part of one of the world's most beautiful cities.

1. There is no place in the world that provides a more historical and dramatic backdrop for a military tattoo than Edinburgh Castle. During the International Festival in August of each year such a tattoo has been held on the Castle esplanade since 1950. This postcard, sent at the turn of the century, shows the Scottish troops on parade on that same esplanade. Edinburgh's famous son, Robert Louis Stevenson, who saw this parade many times in his beloved city, wrote of it when living thousands of miles away on the Pacific Island of Samoa: 'You may see the troops marshalled on the high parade.' Since writing these words, over a century ago, millions have seen the troops on parade at the world's premiere Tattoo on this ancient site.

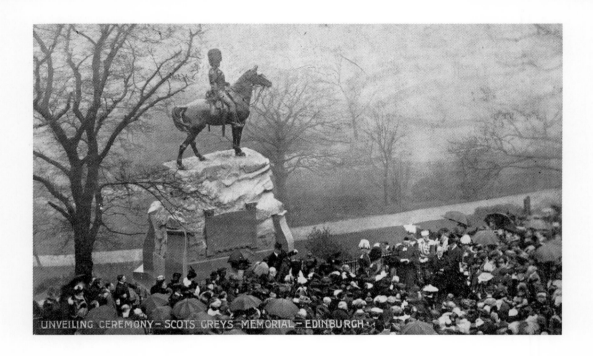

UNVEILING CEREMONY - SCOTS GREYS MEMORIAL - EDINBURGH

2. The handsome memorial, seen in this postcard, was unveiled on 16th November 1906 by Lord Rosebery, to commemorate those Royal Scots Greys who fell in battle. The soldier on horseback is dressed in the uniform of the Scots Greys as they left Edinburgh, in 1899, to fight in the South African war. Judging from this misty scene, and the number of umbrellas among the crowd gathered for the ceremony, it must have been a very wet November day.

EDINBURGH CASTLE, MONS MEG.

3. Mongs Meg, as this cannon is named, was forged in 1476 at Mons, France and at the time of its construction was one of the largest cannons in the world. It was used successfully in many battles until 1682. In that year it burst because of too large a charge when it was fired in honour of the Duke of York. For many years Mons Meg was held in London, but as a result of a campaign by Sir Walter Scott, it was returned to Edinburgh Castle in 1829. The mighty cannon once stood on the ramparts, but because of the damp weather conditions of Edinburgh, it is now housed in a special purpose-built room for its preservation and protection.

The Argyle Tower, Edinburgh Castle

4. Edinburgh Castle is entered by Argyll Tower and Portcullis Gate illustrated in this postcard. The gate was erected by David II and it was here that the two Argylls, father and son, were imprisoned prior to their execution in 1661 and 1685 respectively. The massive construction of this magnificent gate made the entrance to Edinburgh Castle practically impregnable. The upper portion was rebuilt but the lower part, directly over the gateway, is the prison where the two Argylls were held.

E.31.

H.M. Office of Works.

EDINBURGH CASTLE, BANQUETING HALL.

5. The Great Hall of Edinburgh Castle was built by James IV in the 16th century and was used by him for state and ceremonial occasions and banquets. One of its finest features is the hammer-beam roof. In 1640 the hall was the meeting place of the Scottish Parliament, and in 1648 Oliver Cromwell was entertained here, but after that the hall was used as a hospital. Extensive restoration work was undertaken in 1892 and this was paid for by the generosity of Edinburgh publisher William Nelson. Princess Louise, representing Queen Victoria, formally opened the magnificent Hall in that same year, and to this day, the Hall can be seen much as it was in 1892.

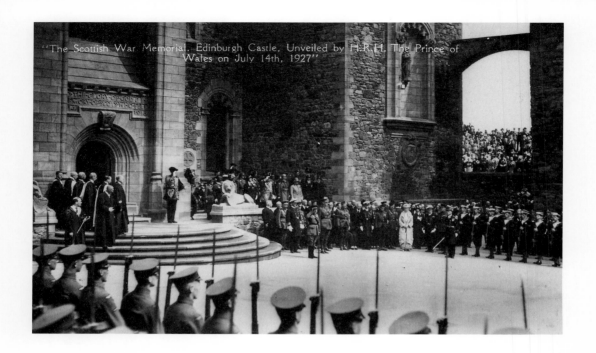

"The Scottish War Memorial, Edinburgh Castle, Unveiled by H.R.H. The Prince of Wales on July 14th, 1927"

6. Upon entering the Scottish National War Memorial at Edinburgh Castle one is immediately impressed by its quiet dignity and peaceful atmosphere and one knows that this is a sacred place; this is a tribute to those responsible for the creation of this beautiful memorial. The basic structure is an 18th century barrack, redesigned by Sir Robert Lorimer, into a memorial that honours 150,000 Scots who died in the First World War. Since then the names of those Scots who lost their lives in the Second World War, have been added in memorial books, that are freely available for inspection by visitors who can look up the names of friends and relations who gave their lives for the Nation. The Memorial was unveiled on 14th July 1927 by the Prince of Wales. His Mother, Queen Mary, can be seen in this picture postcard. This memorial is, without doubt, one of the finest and most dignified of its kind in the world.

NORTH END OF SHRINE, SHOWING STEEL CASKET (PRESENTED BY KING GEORGE & QUEEN MARY.) SCOTTISH NATIONAL WAR MEMORIAL, EDINBURGH CASTLE. 204710.

7. This altar named the 'Shrine' is situated at the very centre of the Scottish National Memorial and stands on the highest point of Castle Rock. On the altar is the casket containing over 150,000 names of Scots who gave their lives in the Great War. Four angels guard the casket. Those who visit this memorial, speak about how moved and inspired they are by the dignity of the place. If the purpose of those responsible for its creation was to uplift and inspire a sense of thanksgiving for those who gave their lives for their country, then that purpose is abundantly fulfilled.

SCOTTISH NATIONAL WAR MEMORIAL, EDINBURGH CASTLE. WROUGHT STEEL CASKET CONTAINING 100,000 NAMES

8. This wrought steel memorial casket is a masterpiece of the metal worker's art and, because of its beauty, is a fitting focal point in the memorial in Edinburgh Castle to those who gave life itself for their country. The memorial casket was the personal gift of King George V and Queen Mary. The only Scottish Queen to have been made a Saint is Queen Margaret and her image can be seen on the front of the casket, with figures of angels holding shields on either side of her. These figures were modelled by Alice Meredith Williams and the master craftsman who wrought the casket was Thomas Hadden.

THE HOSPITAL, EDINBURGH CASTLE.

9. Edinburgh Castle was a self-sustaining community with provision for all the needs of its inhabitants. The Military Hospital on the left, built in 1898, had accommodation for over forty soldiers. The Argyle Battery is in the foreground and a magnificent view of the skyline of Edinburgh can be seen from these ramparts. The Castle, after the Tower of London, is the tourist attraction most visited in Britain. In this picture some of those visitors, even in Edwardian times when this photograph was taken, can be seen in the area near the guns. One young man is captured by the camera looking over the wall at the visitors and nearby is a small cemetery for dogs. (See postcard No. 11.)

A.19. EDINBURGH CASTLE.
Half-Moon Battery
Firing of 1 O'clock gun.

Ministry of Works.

10. Public demand arose in the middle of last century for an accurate time service. The time ball on the top of Nelson's Monument, on Calton Hill, was installed. For many years this time ball set off the cannon on the Half Moon Battery on the ramparts of Edinburgh Castle by electrical controls and this postcard shows this happening. Even today the citizens of the city are very familiar with the firing of the gun and you will often see them around the town checking their watches for accuracy at one o'clock when the gun goes off. The blast of the cannon can be a startling experience, one that frequently shocks unsuspecting visitors. The control clock can be clearly seen in this postcard next to the cannon. This mechanism was made by the famous Edinburgh clock makers James Ritchie and Son (see No. 40.)

11. In the Castle grounds, near St. Margaret's Chapel, the castle's oldest building, there is a small cemetery that should not be missed by the visitor. It is the burial ground for dogs belonging to soldiers that gave faithful service to their masters. It is fitting that 'man's best friend' is remembered and honoured in this way, for there is no doubt that these animals made a significant contribution to the victory and peace that followed the world wars.

A.7. EDINBURGH CASTLE.
View from S. Ramparts.

Ministry of Works

12. This unusual view of the Grassmarket, below the Castle, was taken from the south ramparts. The Grassmarket was a place noted last century as a centre of murder and intrigue. It was the abode of the infamous murderers Burke and Hare who lured their victims to their dwellings, murdered them and then sold their bodies to Dr. Knox at the University for his anatomy classes. Some of the buildings seen in this picture postcard have disappeared to make way for more modern development at a time when town planning and the care of historic buildings were not such a priority as they are today.

13. Born in Edinburgh, Earl Douglas Haig, (1861-1928) was honoured and raised to the peerage for his services in the First World War by a grateful nation. To this day he remains, for many, a national hero. During his lifetime, however, controversy and animosity clouded his reputation because of his dislike and distrust of the Prime Minister, Lloyd George, in particular and politicians in general. It was the ordinary people who thought so highly of him that, by national subscription, they raised enough money to purchase Memersyde Estate and presented it to him as his home. Earl Haig instituted 'Poppy Day' and was largely responsible for the formation of the Royal British Legion for the welfare of ex-service men. This statue on Edinburgh Castle esplanade was not erected by the Scots, but by a grateful man from Bombay, Sir Dhunjibhoy Bomanji.

EDINBURGH CASTLE *H. M. Office of Works*
ESPLANADE, EARL HAIG STATUE

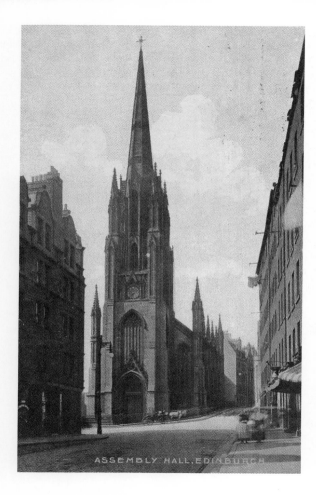

ASSEMBLY HALL, EDINBURGH

14. Victoria or Assembly Hall was built to a design by Gillespie Graham in the Lawnmarket at the junction of Johnson Terrace and Castle Street for the meetings of the General Assembly of the Church of Scotland. Construction of this building that dominates the skyline of Edinburgh began in 1842, but was not finished until two years later. It was also known as Tolbooth St. John's Highland Kirk and it served Tolbooth parish and the Gaelic speaking people of Edinburgh. Today it is used for none of these purposes and the General Assembly meets across the street in the Halls of the former United Free Church of Scotland at New College. The tall spire of this impressive building and its prominent location on Castle Hill make it one of the city's most conspicuous landmarks that can be seen from almost every direction.

A Glimpse of Old Edinburgh

15. The building in this picture has disappeared, but it once stood on the corner of High Street and George IV Bridge and was the home of 'Edinburgh Rock', the famous product of confectioner Alex Ferguson. Alex Ferguson claims in an advert on the building that he had the 'safest sweetmeats'. On the day when this photograph was taken the shop was closed because of a parade and this can be seen in the postcard. Across the street on the right stands Deacon Brodie's Pub and only a few yards away is St. Giles' Cathedral. The site of Alex Ferguson's shop has completely changed today. A modern building, housing local government offices, has replaced the old and seems to be out of place in such a historic setting. 'Edinburgh Rock' confection, however, is still a favourite gift from 'Auld Reekie', the capital of Scotland.

St. Giles' Cathedral, Edinburgh. Where Jenny Geddes flung her Cutty Stool.
Founded about 1120. Restored 1878.

RELIABLE SERIES.

16. Built between the 12th and 15th centuries, St. Giles' Cathedral is the second oldest building in Edinburgh. The Castle is the oldest building. Following the Reformation, St. Giles became Presbyterian and all symbols of Catholicism were removed and destroyed. From 1559 until 1572 the great Scottish Reformer John Knox was its distinguished Minister. In 1637, when King Charles made the church an Episcopal Cathedral, Jenny Geddes, who objected strongly to this change, threw her stool at the head of Dean Hannay as he read the liturgy. This is an event that the Scots have not forgotten and they are proud of the actions of this simple but brave woman, who exercised her freedom to express her sincerely held point of view. Many happenings of great historical importance have taken place in this, the premier Church of Scotland. The Order of the Thistle, an honour given to distinguished citizens of the realm, takes place in the presence of the Sovereign in the Thistle Chapel inside this Cathedral.

JOHN KNOX'S PULPIT,
JENNY GEDDES' STOOL,
REPENTANCE STOOL.

KNOX SERIES.

17. The two items of great historical importance seen in this postcard are in the Royal Museum of Scotland on Queen Street. There isn't much left of the pulpit, but this is the original from which Scotland's greatest reformer, John Knox, preached his fiery sermons at St. Giles' Cathedral in the 16th century. After 450 years it is amazing that so much of the pulpit still survives. Standing in front of the pulpit is a repentance stool, said to be the very stool that Jenny Geddes threw at the Episcopalian Divine Dean Hannay, when he read from the Episcopal liturgy in her Presbyterian Church.

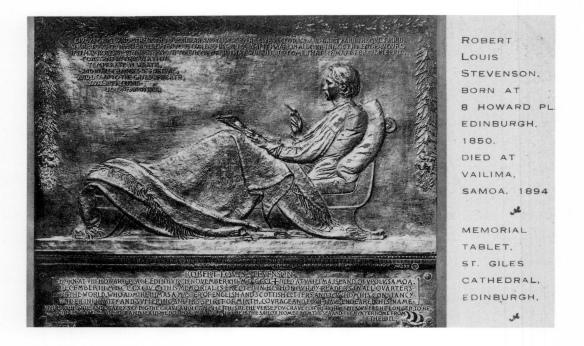

ROBERT
LOUIS
STEVENSON.
BORN AT
8 HOWARD PL.
EDINBURGH.
1850.
DIED AT
VAILIMA.
SAMOA. 1894

MEMORIAL
TABLET.
ST. GILES
CATHEDRAL,
EDINBURGH.

18. One of Edinburgh's most loved writers, Robert Louis Stevenson, was born in 1850 in the capital city at 9 Howard Place. He is honoured on a memorial tablet in St. Giles' Cathedral. He came from a famous family of lighthouse engineers and he himself studied engineering at Edinburgh University before turning to the law. He became an advocate in 1875. It was as a writer of poem and novels, however, that he earned his living and won him world wide fame. Plagued all of his life with lung infections he was forced to find more suitable warmer climates. He left his beloved home city in 1888 and chartered a yacht to sail the Pacific where he visited Tahiti, Hawaii, Gilbert Islands, Samoa and Australia. As a result of these travels he settled, with his American wife Fanny Osbourne, in Samoa, where he built his home, farmed his estate and wrote until his death in 1894.

City Chambers, Edinburgh

19. This is the premier Mercat Cross in Scotland and it stands in front of the City Chambers on the Royal Mile. Most Scottish towns have their own Mercat Cross, where proclamations are made and memorial wreaths often laid, but it was also a place for public sales and purchases for the merchants of Edinburgh. This cross was restored by Gladstone in 1885, but Royal proclamations have been made from this place for centuries. It was also at this spot that Lord Darney professed his innocence of Rizzio's murder at Holyrood Palace, less than a mile away, and where Bothwell was accused of that same murder. Only a short distance away many were executed, including the two Argylls, both father and son, and the Marquis of Montrose. If this historic Mercat Cross could speak, it would be able to recall being witness to many of the events of a great nation. Just a few feet below this cross is Mary Kings' Close, one of Edinburgh's famous 'Closes', which in the 18th century was closed because of the plague. Although hidden from view, it still remains today in its original condition, with shops and houses left as they were 200 years ago. By special arrangement visits to this historic 'time capsule' can be made.

20. Across the street from the Tron Church, on the corner of High Street and Cockburn Street, stands the Cockburn Temperance Hotel, which can be seen in this picture postcard. This hotel no longer exists, but the street still bears the name of the distinguished advocate, Henry, Lord Cockburn, 1777-1854, whose 'Memorial' gave a valuable picture of life in Edinburgh during his lifetime. The Cockburn Association, founded in 1875, named after this public spirited man, keeps a watchful and protective eye upon the amenities of the city.

21. On Hogmanay, thousands gather each year in front of this church to 'bring-in' the New Year as the clock strikes midnight. This ancient church gets its name from the Salt Trone, a pillar with a weighing beam that once occupied this site at the top of Blair Street. Construction of the church began in 1637 to the design of Mylne, the same master mason who built what is referred to as the modern part of Holyrood Palace. Because of a shortage of money the church was not completed until 1644. Nineteen years later the spire was added to the structure, but did nothing for the appearance of the building, which from its beginning looked out of proportion. When South Bridge was built nearby, a part of the east side of the church was taken down to make room for the new roadway. This alteration did not add to the beauty of the building. In 1824 'The Great Fire of Edinburgh' destroyed the spire and part of the church and, although restoration took place and the spire was replaced, the general appearance and proportion of this prominent building on the Royal Mile were not improved and the historic church lost out again on two counts.

TRON CHURCH EDINBURGH.   KNOX SERIES.

MOROCCO LAND, CANONGATE.   KNOX SERIES.

22. Above the door, at Morocco Land in the Canongate, is the tur-
baned head of an African that can be seen in this old postcard.
There is a legend concerning the reason this strange figure appears
on this building and the equally strange name it bears. The legend is
about a young lady from Edinburgh who was on a voyage with Afri-
cans, who sold her to the harem of the Emperor of Morocco. This
Scottish 'lassie' soon became one of his favourites. The girl,
however, always thought of her home in Scotland and often wrote
to her family. This led to her brother establishing a business that
imported merchandise from Morocco. This business flourished and
it was out of that fortune he was able to build Morocco Land on the
Royal Mile in the Canongate.

23. Edinburgh has always been a city of culture, music and entertainment, where theatres, cinemas and concert halls have existed since early times. The Edinburgh International Festival, which began in 1944, is recognised as one of the most outstanding music, art, and drama festivals in the world, where visitors come each year to see outstanding productions and concerts. Many young stars began their careers at this Festival. The city, however, as long ago as 1815, according to Lord Cockburn, had its first music festival in Parliament House. Playhouse Close on the High Street, seen in this postcard, dates back to 1633 and on the site opposite stood Edinburgh's first theatre. In 1756 a production of John Home's play 'Douglas' was performed at the theatre. Reverend Home was the Minister of Athelstaneford Parish in East Lothian and dealt in his play with the issue of the clergy, who frowned upon the theatre.

OLD PLAYHOUSE CLOSE, CANONGATE.
KNOX SERIES

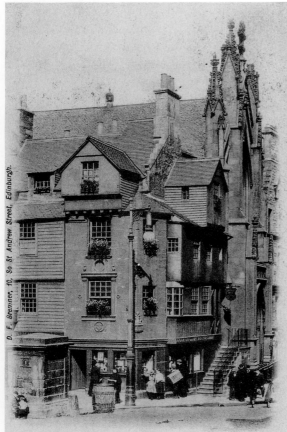

John Knox's House, Edinburgh. RELIABLE WB SERIES.

24. On the Royal Mile there stands the oldest pre-reformation dwelling house in the city, which was the Manse of Scotland's 16th century Protestant reformer, John Knox, who died on 24th November 1572. This ancient residence survived the partial destruction of Edinburgh by the troops of Henry VIII in 1544 and formed part of the dowry of Mariota Arres on her marriage in 1556 to James Mosman, Queen Mary's goldsmith, whose zeal in the Queen's cause cost him his head and his fortune. Above its entrance is an old effigy of Moses receiving the Ten Commandments on Mount Sinai. The outside staircase is typical of Old Edinburgh and many of the fishing communities around the Firth of Forth still have this unusual form of outside staircase. Beside John Knox House can be seen the spires of Knox Church, that was built in 1850 by the Free Church in honour of the reformer. This church no longer exists.

25. This rare and unusual postcard, in the form of a ticket of admission, dates from the turn of the century, when the entrance fee for John Knox House was 6 pence. It was the bright idea of William Hay, who was the custodian of the premises. He had a very keen commercial mind and advertised his personal business on the back of the ticket. His advert states: 'Visitors on leaving John Knox's House by the Old Stair, which formed the original main entrance, are welcome to inspect the unique stock of books, Curiosities, Antiquarian and Artistic Souvenirs, Postcards, etc. for Sale by Mr. Hay, who manages the business. Mr. Hay's Pictorial Postcards are largely his own production and printed in Edinburgh. Lantern Slides of Old Edinburgh are also a special feature.'

John Knox's Hovse, High St., EDINBVRGH

The only Pre-Reformation Dwelling-House in Edinburgh now preserving its original architectural features.

OPEN DAILY from 10 a.m. to 5 p.m.
(Not Open on Sundays)
—WILLIAM J. HAY, *Custodian.*

ADMISSION SIXPENCE.

Voucher No. J 1032

IOANNES CNOXVS

Knox Series.

26. John Knox, 1502-1572, had a profound influence upon the life of the nation in the 16th century and, 400 years later, his influence is still felt. At an early age he was ordained a priest, but soon rejected Catholicism when he came under the influence of the English reformer George Wishart, who visited East Lothian in 1545. The following year Wishart was executed for his beliefs and this made such an impression upon Knox that he became a Protestant minister and teacher at St. Andrews. While working there he was captured by the French, made a galley slave, but was released in 1548 at the request of Edward VI. The King took great interest in Knox and was very active in the English Reformation. In 1560 Knox's Book of Discipline outlined a church constitution on a national plan, with education from parish school to university and help for the poor. This had a profound effect upon education in Scotland and one of the main reasons why the standard of education in the nation has always been very high and played such an important part in the lives of its citizens. In that same year the General Assembly of the Church of Scotland met for the first time. John Knox was then appointed Minister of St. Giles, Edinburgh, where he served until his death in 1572.

27. The Netherbow Port, as it once was seen on the High Street of the Old Town, was built in 1513 but greatly damaged thirty years later by the Earl of Hertford when he attacked Edinburgh. We are fortunate to have this reproduction of a street in Old Edinburgh of the 17th century. This was a feature of the Great Exhibition of 1886, held on the Meadows in the capital city. Netherbow Port was the entrance to this exhibit, where 44 buildings were recreated exactly as they were several hundred years before, so that the public could see Old Edinburgh that had long before disappeared. It was intended that his feature of the Great Exhibition would remain as a permanent exhibit, but this was not to be and it was destroyed after it closed. Netherbow Port was once a fashionable part of town, but it knew the turbulent years of past centuries as well. World's End Close, next to it, was so named because it marked the boundary of the Old Town until 1856, when the Burgh of Canongate became part of the city. Today, on the original site there is the fine Netherbow Arts Centre, that makes this area, once again, an interesting and informative part of Old Edinburgh.

Marshall Wane & Co., No. 58 (Copyright).

The Nether Bow,   Old Edinburgh

Marshall Wane & Co., No. 57 (Copyright).

The Tolbooth, Old Edinburgh.

28. When this postcard was first discovered no one recognised the Tolbooth and it created a mystery. The mystery was solved when it was discovered that one street with 44 shops was recreated exactly as they were in the 17th century at the Great Exhibition on the Meadows in 1886. It was intended that this street of Old Edinburgh would remain, but an act of Parliament forbids all permanent buildings within the Meadows and only Prince Albert's sundial and the Masons' Memorial Pillars remain today. It is, however, fortunate that we have these rare postcards to show us how Old Edinburgh looked like in former days.

29. This ancient building in the Canongate on the Royal Mile was built in 1628 by Countess Mary of Home and was the town residence of the Home and Moray families. Oliver Cromwell used it as his residence when in Edinburgh. From the balcony, on his wedding day, the Earl of Argyll saw Montrose led up the Canongate to his execution. It was in the garden summerhouse of this ancient residence that the Commissioners met to sign the Articles of Union that united England and Scotland. Today, Moray House is the training college for teachers. It passed from the United Free Church, in 1907, to Edinburgh Council, Department of Education.

MORAY HOUSE, CANONGATE.   "KNOX SERIES".

Marshall Wane & Co. No. 3 (Copyright).

French Ambassador's Chapel and House. Old Edinburgh.

30. Here is another postcard of an old Edinburgh building that disappeared years ago. This is how it looked in the 17th century and it comes from the reproductions of an old town street at the Great Exhibition of 1886 and is the French Ambassador's Chapel and house on the High Street. The people standing outside the Chapel are attendants at the Exhibition, in period dress, selling souvenirs to the thousands of visitors who went each day to the Meadows in 1886. This rare postcard was sent from Edinburgh in 1905, many years after the Great Exhibition, and this indicates just how popular this feature was for the people of Edinburgh and visitors to the Exhibition.

31. The Tolbooth, pictured in this postcard, is still in existence on the Royal Mile, but is not the original Tolbooth of Edinburgh which is illustrated in postcard No. 28. This building houses a very interesting museum called The Peoples Story, a new concept, that tells in a graphic and visual way about the times and life of people in the Edinburgh area. On display, with sound, are exhibits of fisher folk, artisans, craftsmen and many other vocations, as well as life in the homes of people of the city. This Tolbooth itself is an historic building and after the Battle of Invercarron, the Marquis of Montrose was imprisoned here prior to his execution on 21st May 1650.

CANONGATE CHURCH, EDINBURGH

ED 140

32. The Canongate Kirk was built in 1688 to accommodate the congregation of the Canongate, when James VII converted the Abbey Church at the Palace of Holyrood into a Roman Catholic Chapel for the Knights of the Thistle. This is the kirk the Sovereign attends when residing at the Palace that is only a few hundred yards away. In the graveyard, behind the church, are buried some distinguished Scots including Adam Smith, author of 'Wealth of Nations', and George Drummond, the much-loved Lord Provost of Edinburgh, elected six times to that office. To this enlightened man the city owes much for its beauty, including the building of the North Bridge, the General Post Office and the development of the New Town. Robert Burns so admired the poet Robert Ferguson, as did Robert Louis Stevenson, that he erected the monument that marks Ferguson's grave in Canongate Kirk Cemetery.

WHITEHORSE CLOSE, CANONGATE. KNOX SERIES.

33. In the 16th century the Royal Mews were located in White Horse Close, illustrated in this postcard. This is how it looked before modern restoration in 1964. Note the outside stairs; a feature of early Edinburgh houses in the Closes of the High Street, also found in the fishing villages around the Firth of Forth. In 1623 Laurence Ord, a merchant of Edinburgh, turned the Royal Mews into a coaching inn and it was from here that coaches left for London; a journey that took more than a week. Ord named the inn 'White Horse' after Mary Queen of Scots' favourite white horse. In 1745, the supporters of Bonnie Prince Charlie used this inn as their headquarters and ale house. In 1798, William Dick, the founder of Edinburgh Veterinary College, more commonly known in the city as the 'Dick Vet', was born here.

QUEEN MARY'S BATH-HOUSE, EDINBURGH. RELIABLE SERIES 340 /

34. This quaint building stands at the bottom of the Royal Mile and that it is ancient, is obvious not only from its appearance, but also from its position on the pavement. Not a lot is known about the building, but it is called Queen Mary's Bath and it could have been used for that purpose by Mary Queen of Scots. A more likely use might be just another cottage on the grounds of the Palace. Near this site was the Physic Gardens, the first planted in Scotland for the promotion of the study of botany and the predecessor of the Royal Botanic Garden, now located in Inverleith Row in the New Town.

HOLYROOD PALACE FROM THE AIR

35. Seen from the air is the Palace of Holyrood House, built in the 15th and 16th centuries by James IV of Scotland (James I of England), on the site of a 12th century Abbey known as the Church of the Holy Cross. This is the official Scottish residence of the British Sovereign when in Scotland. The history of Scotland is closely linked with this Royal Palace. In 1566, David Rizzio, the Italian Secretary of Mary Queen of Scots, was murdered in her presence by her jealous husband, Lord Henry Darnley. David Rizzio advised Queen Mary not to give Darnley the crown and he became so enraged with jealousy that he murdered him. The setting in Queen's Park at the foot of the Royal Mile is breathtaking. Each year in June the Sovereign, during annual visits to Edinburgh, holds a garden party in the beautiful grounds of the Palace, to honour invited guests.

THE KING
Royal Review, Edinburgh, 18th September 1905.

36. This postcard shows King Edward VII on horseback dressed in his Field Marshall's uniform at Holyrood Palace ready to begin the Royal Review held on 18th September 1905. This was one of the greatest military displays ever to be held in the city. The magnificent Review was held in Holyrood Park, today named Queen's Park, behind the Palace, when nearly 40,000 Scottish volunteers paraded past their King.

37. Every year in May, the General Assembly of the Church of Scotland meets at the top of the Mound at the Assembly Hall for the annual meeting. In former times a Scottish nobleman was appointed as Lord High Commissioner to represent the Sovereign, but today the High Commissioner could just as well be a lady. For a fortnight during the Assembly, Holyrood Palace is the residence of the High Commissioner. This picture shows the Lord High Commissioner, last century, on his way to the Assembly Hall from the Palace passing Calton Jail. This building disappeared years ago and was replaced in 1939 by the Art Deco St. Andrew's House, the headquarters of the government in Scotland.

Edinburgh — *The Royal High School*

Waverley Series

38. The Royal High School, whose motto is 'Musis Respublica Floret' (a country flourishes by its culture) has an ancient and distinguished history dating back to 1128, when it was founded as a school of learning by the Abbots of Holyrood. This postcard shows the Doric style building, located at the foot of Calton Hill. It was designed by a former pupil, Thomas Hamilton, and construction began in 1825. It is generally regarded as one of the best of the city's classical buildings. In the mid-1960's the school moved to more modern buildings on East Barnton Avenue in the suburbs of the city. The unused Regent Street building has been remodelled in anticipation of a Scottish Parliament which, to date, has never happened. Recently this building was purchased by Edinburgh Corporation and, should there ever be a Scottish Parliament, the former Royal High will, no doubt, be its home.

Royal High School, Edinburgh.

39. This postcard shows a classroom at the turn of the century, in the Royal High School. Many distinguished pupils have sat in similar classrooms at this distinguished school and among them are Alexander Graham Bell, inventor of the telephone; Sir Walter Scott, novelist; James Naysmith, inventor of steam engines; and most recently Ronnie Corbett, television comedian and personality. The school can also claim that it educated an Anglican Archbishop of Canterbury and a Roman Catholic Archbishop.

Nelson Column, Calton Hill, Edinburgh

40. On Calton Hill is this 106 feet high tower called Nelson's Column. It looks like a telescope and is a monument built to honour the great navy hero Lord Horatio Nelson. The view from the top is spectacular. One of the interesting features of the Nelson Monument can be seen on the top and is called the time ball. In times past, five days a week, a boy from James Ritchie and Son, watch and clock makers, went up to Calton Hill, at 10 minutes to 1 p.m., and raised the ball up the pole. At 1 o'clock it dropped and by electrical connections running to Edinburgh Castle, a time gun was triggered and the gun signalled the exact time. Originally it was installed to allow ships on the Forth to see and record the correct time. Today Edinburgh still has its 1 o'clock time signal when the gun on the Castle ramparts is still fired, but by more modern methods.

14ᵗʰ May – 1903.   *Edinburgh. –*

41. King Edward VII and Queen Alexandra ride though the commemorative arch at Waterloo Place in May 1903 to the Palace of Holyrood House. On the arch is the message 'Edinburgh Hails Her King and Queen'. Hundreds of well-wishers line the street to welcome the King and Queen to the capital of Scotland on their Royal visit and to mark the occasion of Edward's coronation in London, the previous year.

Telegrams - BRITISH, EDINBURGH.
Telephones - 8966-8972 Central.

NORTH BRITISH STATION HOTEL Edinburgh

42. Standing like a giant sentinel above Waverley Railway Station on the corner of Princes Street and The Bridges, is the North British Hotel, the pride and joy of the North British Railway Company, and for many years one of the top five hotels in Britain. This was the northern terminus of the North British east coast line. The imposing building still stands today, recently restored and renamed the 'Balmoral Hotel'.

43. Edinburgh, seen from Calton Hill, is a beautiful sight and it is not difficult to see why 'Auld Reekie', as the capital is affectionately called by many of its inhabitants, is also called the 'Athens of the North'. On the extreme right in this picture postcard is Princes Street. This is, without doubt, one of the most unusual and beautiful streets of any capital city in the world. Like a sleeping giant the ancient castle looks down upon Princes Street with gardens on one side and shops on the other. In the foreground is Calton Jail, a building that disappeared years ago. The obelisk, built in 1845, is in the old Calton burial grounds and is a memorial to the 'Chartist Martyrs' and is only a few steps away from the tomb of David Hume, the greatest of Scotland's philosophers. Also in this cemetery is a monument erected in memory of Abraham Lincoln, the first to the great American President in the United Kingdom. This memorial, with an impressive bronze statue of Lincoln, also honours those Scots who fought in the American War of Independence.

CALTON HILL & NELSON MONUMENT, EDINBURGH.

44. Second only to Edinburgh Castle, Calton Hill commands views of the city that amaze those who view the skyline of Edinburgh from it. This is only one of many hills in the city. On its summit is a creation that looks like a part of the Parthenon called 'Calton's Folly', but its official name is the National Monument. It started as a memorial to the Scots who were killed in the Napoleonic Wars, but was never finished because the money for it ran out. Nelson's Column can be seen to the right and prominent, slightly left of centre, is a round arcade built as a memorial to the philosopher Dugald Stewart. The Old Royal Observatory is seen behind the Steward Memorial.

N.B. Station Hotel, North Bridge, and "Scotsman" Offices, Edinburgh

45. Everywhere you look in Edinburgh there is an impressive view and this postcard shows one of them. The North British Hotel can be seen on the left, the North Bridge in the middle, and to the right the offices of Edinburgh's famous newspaper the 'Scotsman', established in 1817. The large expanse of glass is the unique Waverley Railway Station, 94 steps below Princes Street. A proposal to build a railway station by the North British Railway Company, was put forward as early as 1843, but the people of Edinburgh objected strongly, because this proposal made it necessary to demolish Trinity College and Hospital that occupied the site and they also objected to railway lines being laid in their beautiful Princes Street Gardens. These objections were overcome by claiming more land from the Fruit Market and lines were laid in 1847. The Waverley Station seen in this postcard was opened around 1890 and is said to be the largest area covered by glass in Europe.

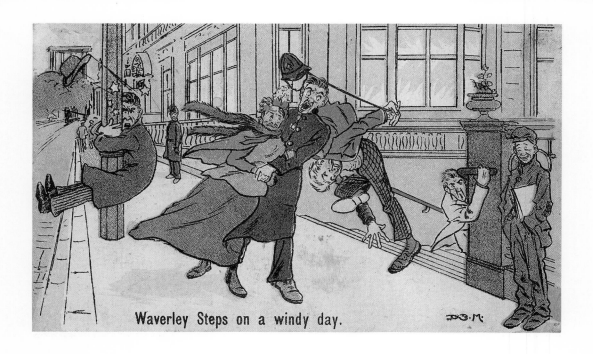

Waverley Steps on a windy day.

46. This comical postcard was sent in 1908 to someone in Greenwich with the message: 'What do you think of this?' Those who have been to Edinburgh by train and walked up the infamous Waverley steps know what this is all about. Such incidents as shown in the postcard are common and are no laughing matter. 'Edinburgh's great enemy', the east wind, funnelling up the long and steep steps is fierce and powerful and is notorious for knocking people off their feet. If you don't believe it try it for yourselves on a windy day and you will soon discover that it takes all your strength to stay upright. Once you have managed to arrive on Princes Street you will be rewarded by a wonderful view of one of the most beautiful streets of any capital city in the world.

ROYAL ARCH PRINCES STREET, EDINBURGH.

NEWINGTON SERIES

47. Royalty are no strangers to the Scottish Capital, in fact, Holyrood Palace, at the foot of the Royal Mile, is their official Palace in Scotland. Balmoral Castle, in Deeside in the Highlands, is their favourite holiday retreat and their love for Scotland is reflected in the frequent visits they make to Balmoral for their annual holiday. This postcard, sent from Edinburgh to Java, is a photograph of the west end of Princes Street with St. John's Scottish Episcopal Church on the left of the arch and through it is seen the Caledonian Hotel. The date was 17th July 1911, when this decorative arch was built to welcome King George V and Queen Mary upon their arrival at the Caledonian Station for their Royal visit to the city.

REGISTER HOUSE AND WATERLOO PLACE, EDINBURGH

8243

VALENTINES SERIES

48. At the east end of Princes Street, at the junction of Leith Street and Waterloo Place, stands the impressive building, seen in the centre of this postcard, known as the 'Waterloo Rooms'. It was the most popular of the amusement halls in Edinburgh at the time it was built. The buildings adjacent to the 'Waterloo Rooms' were, last century, among the finest hotels in the city. The person who sent this postcard has indicated that the building with the flag flying was named Darlings and may well have been one of these hotels. Further along can be seen splendid pillars and arches that are on both sides of the road and surmount the ledges of Regent Bridge. The handsome building on the far left in this picture is Register House, where the records of the nation are kept and where, if you have Scottish ancestors, you can trace your family tree.

49. At the turn of the century, when this postcard was sent, occupying the corner across the street from the North British Hotel, was Stephen's Crown Hotel. Notice also the building next to it named 'Renton's Ltd.'. This was an old department store where ladies and gentlemen, after shopping, could take afternoon tea in splendid surroundings. This corner of Princes Street, next to Register House, has seen dramatic changes over the years and the Crown Hotel has disappeared. For many years it was the home of Woolworths, but today it is 'international' and is known as The Burger King!

GENERAL POST OFFICE EDINBURGH

50. The foundation stone of the General Post Office building in Edinburgh, designed in the Italian style by Robert Matheson, was laid by the Prince Consort, Prince Albert on 23rd October 1861 on the site of the Old Theatre Royal known as Shakespeare Square. It was opened for business in 1866. Long before that date, in 1706, the whole postal service in Edinburgh was managed by four officials and three letter carriers and the place of business was an ordinary shop belonging to the Main family said to be relations of Jenny Geddes (see cards No. 16 and 17). The Penny Post was started in 1776 by Peter Williamson and was so successful it was soon taken over by the government. In 1835 the postmaster was instructed to provide a postal service between London and Edinburgh that took no longer than six days. Today letters sent from Edinburgh by first class post to London are guaranteed next day delivery. This prompt service is extended to many cities and towns throughout Britain. The postal service, which began in such humble circumstances in a small shop in the High Street 200 years ago, has grown and become one of the finest in the world.

51. One of the most prominent sights on Princes Street is George Meikle Kemp's gothic tower, inspired by Melrose Abbey and known as the Scott Monument, dedicated on 15th August 1846 in honour of Edinburgh's great literary son Sir Walter Scott. Seated inside the tower is a statue of the advocate and author with his pet dog Maida. The monument was the result of a competition, in 1836, which Kemp, a joiner and draftsman, won. The choice of his design caused a great deal of controversy and when Charles Dickens came to Edinburgh in 1841, as a member of the Monument Committee, he disapproved of the final result of the tribute to his friend, Sir Walter Scott, and wrote in the London Morning Chronicle: 'I am sorry to report the Scott Monument a failure. It is like the spire of a Gothic church taken off and stuck into the ground.' The Monument has on it figures of 64 characters from Scott's novels and 16 statuettes of Scottish poets. From the top reached by 287 steps are spectacular views of city. The Monument originally cost £16,000 but recent restoration cost £154,000.

Scott Monument   Edinburgh

"North British Railway Series."

M.W.&Co.,E.

Scott's Statue, Edinburgh. (Hardie)

52. Seated inside the Scott Monument is the twice life-size statue of Sir Walter Scott and his pet dog Maida by the sculptor Sir John Steell. This beautiful work of art is carved from a solid block of Carrara marble from the Italian Apennines in Tuscany and was the first marble statue in Scotland. When it is illuminated each evening it is an impressive sight.

Old Town from Scott's Monument,
Edinburgh.

53. This picture was taken from the top of the Scott Monument and shows the Old Town with Waverley Railway Station in the foreground. St. Giles' Cathedral spire, a crown that has a recorded history as old of the High Street itself and the chief ornament of Old Edinburgh, can be seen on the right. Nearby St. Giles are the Council Chambers, long ago known as the Royal Exchange and built in 1753. This building can be seen at the end of Waverley Bridge and rises to a height of 12 stories. Edinburgh claims that this was the first skyscraper in the world and this postcard seems to support that claim.

54. So impressed was the great Victorian writer William Thackeray with Edinburgh that when he saw Princes Street for the first time, he described it as 'in truth a promenade for Princes'. Many today would describe Princes Street Gardens with its unsurpassed views as 'in truth a garden for Kings and Queens'. It is not only the Castle that makes Edinburgh uniquely beautiful, but also its hills, its classical architecture, the Firth of Forth and the Old and New Towns. This is a view of the band stand in Princes Street Gardens and you can see that the people of Edinburgh have gathered to hear the military band playing. This was a popular entertainment at the time this postcard was produced at the turn of the century, but that custom continues today and each summer people still gather in Princes Street Gardens to enjoy the concerts there, not at the bandstand, but in an outdoor theatre covered over by a gigantic tent.

55. Where Littlewoods Store stands today on Princes Street once stood R. and T. Gibson, high class family grocers. This photograph shows that same shop in 1935. In those days people received personal attention from the staff and the customer was the most important part of the business. Those were the days when you could see, feel and even sample what you intended to purchase. With the coming of large multinational shops like Marks and Spencer, Littlewoods and British Home Stores, excellent though they may be, personal service all but disappeared and shops like Gibson's found themselves unable to compete. Notice the sign advertising dragees for sale at 2 shillings a pound. Dragee is a Victorian word for chocolate sweetmeat and silver balls for decorating cakes and confection.

STATUE of the REVd THOMAS GUTHRIE, D.D.:-
PRINCES STREET, EDINBURGH. →

THOMAS GUTHRIE
D.D.

PREACHER · PHILANTHROPIST

1803-1873

56. Although Dr. Thomas Guthrie was a native of Brechin, born in 1803, he was one of the 'saints' of the poor children of Edinburgh and devoted to their cause. He studied at Edinburgh University and was ordained in 1825. He then studied surgery and anatomy with the famous anatomist Dr. Robert Knox of 'Burke and Hare' fame, before going to Paris University to continue his medical studies. A man of deep compassion he always identified himself with the poor, oppressed and underprivileged. The vice and degradation of Paris left a permanent impression on him and he came back to Edinburgh to serve at Old Greyfrias Kirk in the Cowgate. At the time of the disruption in the Church of Scotland he was one of the leaders of the new Free Kirk. When he became Minister of St. John's Free in the West Bow it was from there that he launched his appeal for a Ragged School System for hundreds of destitute children who roamed the street of Edinburgh. He offered education, clothing and training. The prison population at Calton Jail was reduced to almost nothing because of the compassionate good work of this great man, who is honoured in Princes Street Gardens by this statue, an honour that Dr. Guthrie greatly deserved.

ASSEMBLY HALL. CHURCH OF SCOTLAND. EDINBURGH   SUTHERLAND

57. This imposing building at the top of the Mound, the work of William Playfair and David Bruce, is New College, but when it was built in 1846-1850, it was the Theological College of the United Free Church until the Union of 1929, when the United Free and the Church of Scotland became one Kirk. Ministers of the Kirk and students from all over the world come to Edinburgh University, New College, for theological training and the author of this book is a post-graduate student from America who stayed in Scotland after his studies at New College to serve as a Minister in a Kirk. The Assembly Hall, where the Church of Scotland meets each May for its annual meeting, stands behind New College on the site of the former Palace of Queen Mary of Guise, widow of James. Mary used this Palace as her residence when the English burned down the Palace of Holyrood in 1544. The buildings to the right of the two towers of New College have been modernised and made into students' quarters and the building to the left is now the Theological College of the Free Church of Scotland, although when this postcard was produced, the lower floor was The Edinburgh Savings Bank.

58. All work and no play makes Jock a poor preacher! Here is a picture of the 1904-1905 season Football Club of the Church of Scotland Training College. These young men, like thousands before and after them, were the heroes of the church who served throughout the length and breath of Scotland and beyond as Ministers, Missionaries and Pastors. Many of them became outstanding preachers and teachers of world renown. Part of the message on the back of this postcard, sent in 1905, says: 'These postcards are 3 a penny – quite cheap!' Perhaps the team did not do so well that year!

PRINCES STREET LOOKING EAST, EDINBURGH.

59. Standing on the corner of Princes Street and the Mound, facing Hanover Street is the Royal Institute or School of Arts, founded in February 1819. It later became the Royal Scottish Academy, where exhibitions of Scottish artists are often held. The present building, like the National Gallery behind it, was designed by William Playfair and its construction began in 1825. It had to be built upon piles because of the instability of the ground, for this area was once covered by the waters of the Nor' Loch, until it was drained to be made into Princes Street Gardens. It is because of beautiful buildings like this Doric temple that Edinburgh is considered by many to be one of the most beautiful cities in the world.

OLD TOWN.   EDINBURGH.

60. Dominating the skyline of the Old Town at the top of the Mound is the Bank of Scotland, seen on the right side of this picture postcard. It was established on 17th July 1695 by an Act of Parliament of Scotland, making it the oldest commercial bank in the United Kingdom. Work on the building began in 1800, when the foundation was laid to designs by Robert Reid and Richard Crichton, who were students of the distinguished Georgian architect Robert Adam. This building was opened on 12th August 1806. By the mid-19th century the banking business expanded to such an extent that the building became too small and had to be enlarged. In 1860 David Bryce, the well-known Edinburgh architect, submitted his plans for enlargement and they were accepted. Since that date the building has been enlarged several times, but remains, on the exterior, faithful to the 1860 design of Bryce, making it a beautiful landmark on the skyline of Edinburgh. One of the highlights of the Christmas decorations of the city is the lighting of this beautiful building.

Edinburgh Castle from Scott Monument,

RELIABLE WB AS SERIES.

61. On the left, below the Castle, is the National Gallery of Scotland designed by William Playfair in 1845. In front of it is the Royal Institute, also designed by Playfair. These two buildings look like twin Grecian temples, but on close inspection one is Doric and the other, The National Gallery, is Ionic. Although not a large building, nor having a large collection, it has, nevertheless, the most important group of Old Masters in Britain outside London. In 1946 the Duke of Sutherland loaned his magnificent collection of Titians, Raphaels and Rembrandts to the gallery, to augment the already outstanding collection on display. Note the coat of arms of the city of Edinburgh on the left hand corner.

62. In 1903 Mr. J.W. M'Hattie, the city gardener, suggested that there should be a floral clock in West Princes Street Gardens. James Ritchie and Son, the famous Edinburgh firm of clock makers, designed and built such a clock out of an old movement from the parish church of Elie, in Fife, and it was first started on 10th June 1903. This was the first floral clock in the world. Today this famous clock in West Princes Street Gardens is imitated around the world. Edinburgh has a long tradition of gardens going back as far as 1670 to the Physic Garden, that eventually resulted in the formation of Royal Botanic in 1820-1823, one of the finest in Britain.

63. Today there are over 1,000 taxis in Edinburgh, but around the turn of the century, when this picture was taken, there were only a few and in the early days of the automobile they were grand cars. The driver is dressed in his uniform waiting for wealthy customers on Princes Street. Although the taxi was expensive even before the automobile, horse-drawn taxis before the advent of this 'new fangled machine' were a common sight on the streets of Edinburgh. Today the public-spirited taxi drivers of the capital city provide, on the second Tuesday in June, an outing to Yellowcraigs near Aberlady in East Lothian, for disabled children and adults. From the hospitals, homes and care centres of the city they pick up their special passengers for the day's outing and assemble at Murrayfield, where the drivers and taxis are judged for the best-dressed cab and driver. Then the huge fleet of taxis, with their happy guests, parade down Princes Street, London Road, though Portobello then on to Luca's famous ice cream shop in Musselburgh, where this generous family provides free ice cream for all on the outing. At Yellowcraigs, a day of fun, with picnics, games, races and prizes, is enjoyed by all.

RAMSAY LODGE, EDINBURGH.

340 / 397

THIS IS A REAL PHOTO

64. Rising like a film set at the top of the Mound, on the north slope of Castle Hill, stands Ramsay Lodge, a unique group of houses that, like the Castle, dominate the skyline of the Old Town. These houses, which command some of the most spectacular views in the city, began in the first half of the 18th century, when Allen Ramsay, the poet, purchased the land on which he built his octagonal-shaped retirement home. In 1745 he left Edinburgh when Bonnie Prince Charlie entered the city. Later, his son the portrait painter, also called Allen, inherited the property. He built three additional houses that were completed in 1768. A statue of the famous poet who first built Ramsay Lodge, known today by many as Ramsay Garden, was erected to honour him in West Princes Street Gardens near the floral clock. It was Patrick Geddes, environmentalist, town planner, and owner of the Camera Obscura, who was most responsible for Ramsay Lodge looking as it does today.

The Scottish American Memorial
in West Princes Street Gardens, Edinburgh

C 813

65. This handsome war memorial entitled 'The Spirit of 1914' in Princes Street Gardens is known as the Scottish American War Memorial and is the work of sculptor Dr. R. Tait Mackenzie of Philadelphia, who took three years to complete his work. It was dedicated by the Scottish American Memorial Committee in 1927. The conception of its design is interesting. Seated on a plinth is a kilted soldier looking toward historic Castle Rock and behind him is a bronze frieze of recruits from all walks of life falling in behind a pipe band. Above this frieze are two intertwined wreaths upon which are the Stars and Stripes of America and the St. Andrew's Cross of Scotland, symbolic of the friendship between the two nations. The architect for this memorial was Mr. Reginald Fairlie of Edinburgh.

66. St. John's Scottish Episcopal Church, at the west end of Princes Street, is a fine Gothic building with some details of St. George's Chapel, Windsor and Westminster Abbey, London, incorporated in its design. The mother of Sir Walter Scott and the Scottish portrait artist Sir Henry Raeburn are buried in vaults below the church. In this postcard is seen also, on the right, St. Cuthbert's Church below the Castle.

EDINBURGH CASTLE FROM LOTHIAN ROAD. 73B. SCOTIA SERIES

67. On the edge of the Nor Loch, below the Castle, stands St. Cuthbert's Church. It has a distinguished and ancient history believed to date back to the 8th century. For a time this church had the largest parish in Midlothian and was responsible for supporting and founding many chapels around the city. The building, pictured here, was built in 1775, and at that time was the largest church in Edinburgh, having two galleries and accommodation for over 3,000 worshippers. This famous church at the West End has a distinguished record of gifted and outstanding ministers and preachers.

Edinburgh Castle, from the West, and Resurrectionist Watch Tower, St. Cuthbert's Churchyard.

Here the citizens, by turns, armed with blunderbusses kept nightly watch to prevent the graves being desecrated by body snatchers or resurrectionists. (See MANSIE WAUGH).

68. Edinburgh Castle is perched high above this tower known as 'Resurrectionist Watch Tower', situated in St. Cuthbert's Churchyard. From this tower citizens of the city took their turn each night, armed with blunderbusses, guarding the graves of their loved ones to prevent them from being desecrated by body snatchers and resurrectionists. This may sound a bit far-fetched, until you realise that this did take place. Only a short distance away in the Grassmarket lived the most famous murderers and body snatchers of all, Burke and Hare, who sold their bodies regularly to Dr. Robert Knox of the University Anatomy Department for his medical students. Perhaps some of the bodies they provide for the professor came from this very cemetery.

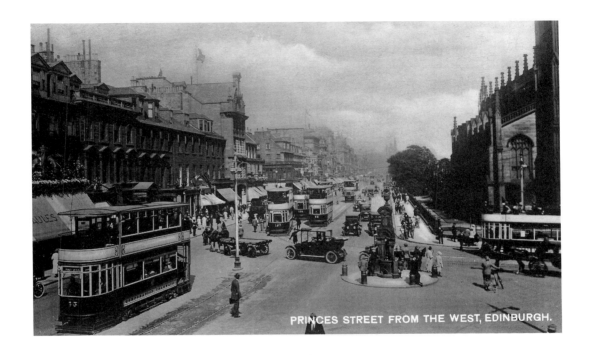

PRINCES STREET FROM THE WEST, EDINBURGH.

69. This photograph shows just how busy Princes Street was the early part of this century. It must have been a tram driver's nightmare as trams turned down Lothian Road to the right or continued straight on to the west end of the city. At this busy intersection at Princes Street and Lothian Road there are not only trams to contend with, but also the 'new' automobiles and many horse-drawn carts. Little has changed, only the vehicles, since this picture was taken almost a hundred years ago, for today the traffic jams are just as bad as ever and Princes is the second busiest shopping street in Britain.

OLD CALEDONIAN STATION 1890

70. This rare postcard shows the station of the Caledonian Railway in 1890, known as Princes Street Station. At the turn of the century this building completely disappeared when the Caledonian Hotel was built on this site and opened in 1903. The station was then entered from the ground level of the hotel and was the terminus of the London Midland and Scottish Railway (LMS). Travellers came to the capital via Carlisle and Carstairs Junction. The LMS followed the old London and North-West Railway from Euston, London, as far as Carlisle and then travelled on the tracks of the Caledonian Railway through the beautiful border country of Scotland, until it reached this station on the west end of Princes Street. Services to and from the Caledonian Station continued until it was closed in 1965.

71. This passageway, called a 'vennel' in Scotland, leads from Lauriston to the Grassmarket and contains a fragment of the ancient wall that was hurriedly built in 1513 to protect the city from invaders after the disastrous Battle of Flodden, when King James lost his life and many Scottish nobles perished. As this postcard illustrates, the Castle is the dominant feature of the Edinburgh skyline and from almost every direction this mighty fortress can be seen.

EDINBURGH CASTLE FROM THE VENNEL.   "KNOX SERIES."

72. The gloomy atmosphere of this old picture of the Grassmarket is appropriate for here intrigue and murder took place and the gallows of the city stood where many of the infamous and famous were hanged. Between 1661 and 1688 over a hundred Covenanters were hanged for their religious beliefs and nearby is a memorial plaque bearing the inscription: 'For the Protestant faith on this spot many Martyrs and Covenanters died.' Not far from that spot is Tanners Close, where William Burke and William Hare, two Irish immigrants, carried out their 'business' of supplying bodies to surgeons for medical research. These two body snatchers, as they were called, were the inspiration for Stevenson's 'Dr. Jekyll and Mr. Hyde'. They lured paupers and prostitutes to their lodgings, strangled them and sold them to Dr. Knox, professor of anatomy, for the use of his medical students. Hare eventually turned against his partner in crime and got away with murder, but on Christmas Eve 1829 Burke was hanged on the Grassmarket gallows. The judge suggested that his skeleton be preserved in remembrance of what he did to his victims. This suggestion was heeded and today Burke's skeleton can be seen at Surgeons Hall.

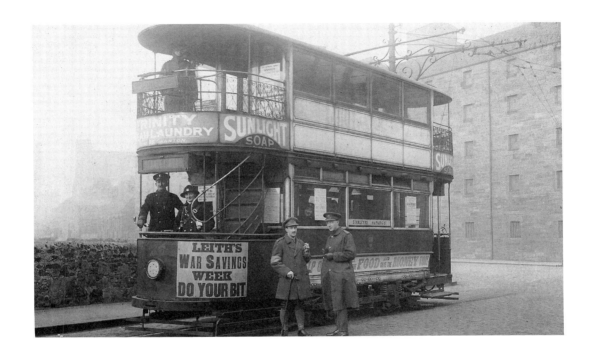

73. From the end of the 19th century until well into the 1950's, trams were a common sight on the streets of the Edinburgh and its surrounding suburbs. This early 'double decker' was one of these trams and you can see by its advertisement for war savings that it saw active service during the First World War on the streets of the capital city. The driver and his conductor are standing at attention while two servicemen look on. Today all of these trams have disappeared and have become treasured museum pieces, however, you can still see a short section of the tram lines by the General Post Office in Waterloo Place preserved, no doubt, as a reminder of 'the good old days'.

74. Only the façade of Theatre Royal is grand at Shakespeare Square. Behind the façade was a barn-like structure described by one writer as 'a blot upon the most important and crowded thoroughfare in Edinburgh'. This famous theatre was demolished in 1861 to make way for the General Post Office. Almost a century before, in 1794, a memorable row was started by several Irish medical students who were in favour of the French Republic. Loyal Scottish students, including Sir Walter Scott, who had just passed his exams to become an advocate, insisted that the musicians should play 'God Save the King', while the audience would stand at attention with heads uncovered. The Irish students would not stand. On the following Saturday both groups returned to the theatre, armed with sticks, to settle their differences, but no one knows the final outcome of this row. The Theatre Royal entertained the people of Edinburgh for generations in many different locations around the city. On another site, in different buildings, the Theatre Royal continued until 1946, when the building was destroyed by fire.

North Bridge.   Edinburgh.

I suppose you have heard of this place

1843. Albany Series.

75. The plan for a bridge over this ravine began with James II, but it was not until 1763, when Lord Provost George Drummond laid the foundation stone for this wonderful North Bridge, that the plane, became a reality and opened up the lands to the north which eventually became the New Town. A hundred years later the bridge had to be widened to accommodate the newly acquired trams that can be seen in this postcard. A new bridge was built at the end of the 19th century to replace the old one and this is the bridge seen in this picture postcard. One of the piers is a sculptured memorial, by Birnie Rhind, RSA, to the officers and men of the King's own Scottish Borderers. This regiment has the exclusive right to march through the streets of the city in peace time with bayonets fixed, because it was this Edinburgh Regiment that was raised in 1688 to defend the city. The building on the right is the Scotsman Newspaper offices and on the left is the Calton Hotel. It is interesting that the bridge continues between these buildings.

Thirty Linotype Composing Machines, "The Scotsman" Offices, Edinburgh.   Valentines Series

76. One of the great Scottish newspapers is the 'Scotsman', established in 1817, and this picture postcard shows the linotype machine room, about 1900, with thirty machines and their operators at work. The lighting of the room is by gas and a hand proofing machine can be seen in the centre foreground. Today all this has changed dramatically in an era when the computer is 'king' and now with a few programmers sitting before their computers, the work of this entire office in 1900 can be done quicker, better, and with only a fraction of the staff.

77. This rare postcard shows the department store Bon Marche at 15 North Bridge, that very few people will remember because it closed in 1906. In that year the site was taken over by Patrick Thomson, who expanded in 1910 to numbers 11, 13, 17, 19 North Bridge and created one of Edinburgh's finest and largest department stores. Afternoon concerts by the Patrick Thomson orchestra, while ladies and gentlemen took their afternoon tea, is still talked about with appreciation by those who remember those more genteel and leisurely days, when shopping was a pleasure to be enjoyed. Unfortunately 'PT's', as they were affectionately known by the people of Edinburgh, are also closed, but the building remains and has become the fine Calton Highland Hotel.

Bon Marché, North Bridge, Edinburgh

Tea Room, Bon Marché, Edinburgh *Does it remind you of Interlaken or Loürche - us - Bains.*

78. Bon Marche also had its tea rooms and they can be seen on this postcard sent in 1904. Taking afternoon tea after shopping or meeting friends in the city has always been an Edinburgh custom that continues to this day and many of the new shops and department stores have tea rooms and restaurants. The lady who sent this postcard has written below the picture this question: 'Does it remind you of Interlaken or Loürche?' (in Switzerland). The sign on the first arch has this notice; 'Coffee and Smoke Room'. It is interesting that as early as 1904 a separate area is provided for those who wished to smoke. This must be one of the earliest instances of this thoughtful idea.

79. On this stage of the Empire Palace Theatre, opened on 7th September 1892, some of the greatest performers of the 20th century have appeared, including Charlie Chaplain, Judy Garland, Moira Shearer, Gracie Fields, Harry Lauder and hundreds of others. One of the most eccentric and popular illusionists at the beginning of this century was 'The Great Lafayette', who opened a two-week season here in May 1911, but disaster struck with the death of his best friend, his pet dog Beauty. Lafayette was brokenhearted and had his dog embalmed and buried in Piershil Cemetery in Portobello with the understanding that he himself would be buried there upon his death. On the evening of 9th May, a few days after the funeral of Beauty, with a lighted torch, Lafayette accidentally set the stage alight and was killed along with ten others. On 14th May the streets of Edinburgh were lined with spectators as they viewed the funeral procession from the parlour on Morrison Street to Piershill Cemetery, where the ashes of Lafayette were placed beside his best friend, Beauty. Today the Empire lives again, after extensive restoration, and it becomes the 'Edinburgh Festival Theatre' when the curtain rises on 18th June 1994.

Augustine Church, George IV. Bridge, Edinburgh. J.R.R.E

80. On George IV Bridge, seen on the right side of this postcard, is Augustine Congregational Church, opened in November 1861. The name of Edinburgh's second Congregational Church was suggested to the Minister, Dr. Lindsay Alexander, by Mr. Sloan, a member of the congregation who reminded his Minister that he often quoted from the works of St. Augustine from the pulpit. Dr. Alexander thumped his hand on his desk and replied: 'Mr. Sloan, Augustine it will be.' This much loved scholar and pioneer of Scottish Congregationalism was one of the most prominent figures in the Scottish Ministry outside the Church of Scotland. He was chosen as one of the panel of British scholars to revise the Authorised Version of the Bible and was a contributor to Encyclopaedia Britannica, which was published in Edinburgh. After his retirement he was principal, for five years, of the Theological Hall that met for a time in rooms below this church, where his powerful influence and scholarship were appreciated by his students, who humorously described themselves as 'cave dwellers' in the sunless room below the Augustine Church.

Public Library, Edinburgh.

81. Like so many other libraries throughout Britain and the United States, Central Library, originally known as Edinburgh Free Library, was the gift of Andrew Carnegie, the weaver's son from Dunfermline, who went to America and became one of the richest men in the world through his Carnegie Steel Company in Pennsylvania. During the later part of his life, he gave away to good causes over $350,000,000 and established more than 2,500 libraries. He laid the foundation stone for this building on 9th July 1887. The view seen on this postcard is misleading, for it only shows the top two floors of a very large building. The foundation is in the Cowgate and the building rises many stories to this entrance on George IV Bridge.

Greyfriars Bobby, Edinburgh.

Collar presented by the Lord Provost.

A TRIBUTE
TO THE AFFECTIONATE FIDELITY OF
GREYFRIARS BOBBY
IN 1858 THIS FAITHFUL DOG FOLLOWED
THE REMAINS OF HIS MASTER TO GREYFRIARS
CHURCHYARD AND LINGERED NEAR THE SPOT
UNTIL HIS DEATH IN 1872

WITH PERMISSION
ERECTED BY THE
BARONESS BURDETT COUTTS

82. Edinburgh has hundreds of statues but none more delightful than the monument erected to honour a dog called 'Greyfriars Bobby'. People from all over the world come to see the water fountain and memorial tablet dedicated to that faithful sky terrier who, from 1858, spent the rest of his life, 14 years, guarding the grave of his humble master Jock, who was buried in the nearby cemetery of Greyfriars Kirk. Baroness Burdett Coutts was so touched by the faithfulness of this dog that she erected this statue and drinking fountain for animals at the junction of Candlemakers Row and George IV Bridge. The Lord Provost of Edinburgh gave Bobby the freedom of the city, and the collar, now in the Huntly House Museum in the Royal Mile, was Bobby's badge of honour. To this day the loyal Bobby has captured the imagination of people all over the world. Books have been written about him and Walt Disney made a film about him that was shown in cinemas the world over, enchanting children and adults alike.

M'Ewan Hall and Students' Union, Edinburgh
Printed by V. and S., Ltd., D., for The Picture Post Card Bureau, Edinburgh

83. McEwan Hall, completed in 1897 to a design by Sir Rowan Anderson at a cost of £115,00, was gifted to Edinburgh University by Sir William McEwan MP, who was chairman of the famous McEwan Brewery, one of Scotland's premier brewers of beer. The interior of this beautiful building is in the form of a Greek theatre and is used for graduation ceremonies, where students from all faculties receive their degrees. I was a guest here when the King of Norway was presented with an Honorary Doctors degree in 1962. Behind the platform is a huge panel, 100 feet long, representing the Temple of Fame, and containing nearly a hundred figures. The organ, one of the finest in the United Kingdom, was built by Hope-Jones. Next to McEwan Hall is the University Student Union, paid for by former students.

ROYAL SCOTTISH MUSEUM, CHAMBERS ST., EDINBURGH.

84. First known as the Museum of Science and Art, then as the Royal Scottish Museum, today it is popularly known as Chambers Street Museum. It was first built for purposes of study by the students of Edinburgh University who entered the museum by a connecting bridge from University buildings in the Old Quad. The building itself on the outside is in a fine Venetian Renaissance style and was the creation of Captain Fowkes. The foundation stone was laid on 23rd October 1861 by Prince Albert and it was opened in 1866. The interior is one of the most beautiful Victorian galleries in the world. It is one of the most important institutions of its kind in the United Kingdom, with departments including scientific instruments, clocks and watches, silver, porcelain, engineering and many others. Its natural history rooms are fascinating to both young and old and this wonderful museum is worth a visit. A new wing is under construction, which has caused a great deal of controversy, because of its very modern appearance, which is a dramatic contrast with this Victorian building.

Heriot-Watt College   Edinburgh

85. Heriot-Watt Technical College was an affiliated college of Edinburgh University, but today it has full University status in its own right and has moved to a new campus, in fine modern buildings, on the outskirts of the city at Riccerton. The College was originally established by the trustees of George Heriot's Trust for students, who wanted an engineering and technical education. The statue, seen in this postcard behind the horse-drawn bus, is that of the famous Scottish inventor of the steam engine, James Watt, after whom the College was named, together with George Heriot, whose estate provided the money.

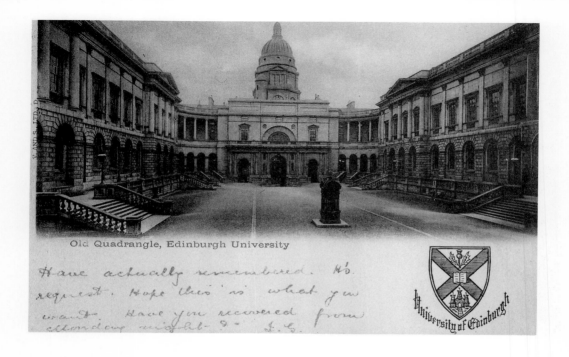

Old Quadrangle, Edinburgh University

Have actually remembered. H's request. Hope this is what you want. Have you recovered from Monday night? — I.G.

University of Edinburgh

86. Although the entrance to the Old Quadrangle of Edinburgh University is the work of Robert Adam in 1789, the buildings inside the Quad are by another famous Edinburgh architect, William Playfair. On the dome can be seen the 'Golden boy', who is carrying the torch of learning and was the creation of Sir Rowan Anderson, who built McEwan Hall. History abounds in this place and it was on this very site that once stood St. Mary's in the Fields, more commonly known as 'Kirk o'Field', that was ripped apart by an explosion that killed Lord Darnley, husband of Mary Queen of Scots on 10th February 1567. On this postcard is the coat of arms of the University comprising the Thistle and St. Andrew's Cross for Scotland, the Castle for Edinburgh and the open book, symbol of learning.

87. This stately building was known as Heriot's Hospital but, as a school for boys, was the gift of George Heriot, called by Sir Walter Scott in 'Fortunes of Nigel' as 'Jingling Geordie'. Heriot was a wealthy banker and a jeweller to James VI, who left his entire estate in trust to the Magistrates and Ministers of Edinburgh for the teaching and maintenance of the sons of poor burgesses. The building was begun in 1628 and designed by Inigo Jones. Cromwell's wounded soldiers were cared for here, although the word 'hospital' was used in Edinburgh for 'school'. In 1787 the gardens were used by an Italian balloonist, Vincenzo Lundardi, when he made his ascent over the Firth of Forth. This was certainly in the earliest days of ballooning in Scotland. Over the years many famous pupils attended Heriot's but none more famous than the poor orphan from the Stockbridge part of the town, who came to study here in 1764 and later became one of Scotland's great portrait painters, Sir Henry Raeburn.

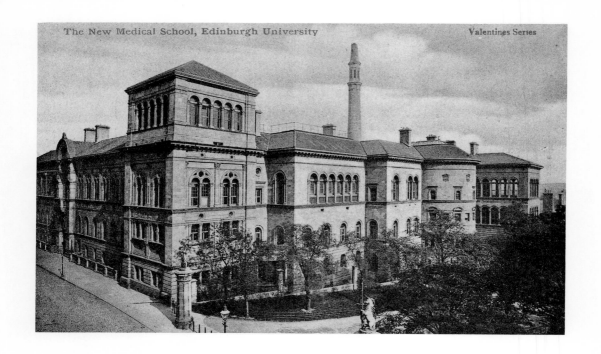

88. By 1874, when this building to a design by Sir Rowan Anderson was begun, the facilities of the Old Quad (see card No. 86) were outgrown by the increased student enrolment and there was need for a purpose-built College of Medicine. When the College was completed it was one of the finest and best-equipped Medical Colleges in Europe and, even today, its students enjoy a reputation of world renown. When it first opened it not only had facilities for the medical faculty but also for law, the arts, and theology. In the medical museum were many interesting exhibits, but none more famous than the skeleton of Burke, the famous murderer and grave robber, and one of his many victims, Daft Jamie. The skeleton of Burke was kept at the suggestion of the judge who sentenced him to be hanged on the Edinburgh Gallows in the Grassmarket. The skeleton of Burke is now in Surgeons Hall.

89. The greatest Institution for the relief of suffering in Edinburgh, The Royal Infirmary, was opened in a small hired house in 1729. Through the efforts of Edinburgh's most outstanding Lord Provost, George Drummond, who was instrumental in raising the money for this venture, this great teaching hospital was built. The foundation stone for the building seen in this postcard was laid by the Prince of Wales in October 1870 and was opened nine years later. The building is of the Scottish Baronial style designed by David Bryce RSA and the work was carried out by his nephew, John Bryce. Many of the world's great physicians and surgeons have been trained here and although needing to be replaced by more modern buildings, this 'Institution for the relief of suffering in Edinburgh' has made outstanding contributions to the care of its patients and in its pioneering work and discoveries in medicine, that has given it a reputation of which the Scots can be justly proud. Kidney and liver transplants are just two modern procedures that were pioneered at this hospital. There are hundreds more that have enhanced and improved the lives of millions.

90. During the commemorate visit of King George V and Queen Mary in 1911, the Royal couple visited the Royal Infirmary and the ward that was named after the Queen. It may look somewhat dated, but you can see that it is spotlessly clean and the patients were cared for by devoted nurses. In 1911 over 12,600 patients were treated in wards, 38,800 patients were treated as outpatients and the daily number of patients in ward was 846. The hospital always admitted patients on the urgency of their need and there was no payment for treatment or care, for it was a National Charity supported by donations. The cost for each patient, per day, in 1911 in the Royal Infirmary was under £5,00.

91. This handsome redstone building on Lauriston Place, opened on 7th June 1900 by Lord Provost Mitchell Thomson, is the Edinburgh Fire Brigade Headquarters, built to replace the old premises on High Street. The famous brigade, now known as the Lothian and Borders Fire Brigade, was formed in 1824, the first in the United Kingdom and one of the first in Europe. Untrained and new, this small band of men had their 'baptism of fire' beginning just weeks after its formation on 15th November of that same year in one of the worst fires in the history of the capital known as 'The Great Fire of Edinburgh'. It began in a printer's workshop on the High Street, spread to tenement after tenement until it reached the spire of Tron Kirk and destroyed it. The fire continued up the High Street and broke out in Parliament Square, when it looked like Old Edinburgh would be completely destroyed. Fortunately on 19th November the weather changed and heavy rain extinguished all the fires. This was the beginning of an outstanding fire service that, over the years had given heroic and distinguished service to Edinburgh and the surrounding countryside all the way to the borders.

Meadow Walk, Edinburgh

92. The Meadows is one of the many beautiful parks in the centre of Edinburgh and, in this picture postcard of about 1910, you can see some of the citizens enjoying a stroll down Meadow Walk. The spires of the Royal Infirmary can be seen in the distance. At one time this area was South Loch of the Old Town and supplied water to the city before pipes were laid to the Pentland Hills to the south of the city, from where it received its water supply. The Meadows has always been used for recreational activities and even today you will see students from the University and nearby schools playing cricket, football, and other sports in this wonderful parkland. One of the charming features of Edinburgh is that it has so many parks and playgrounds. In 1886 the International Exhibition of Science and Art was held in the Meadows and this was the first international exhibition to be held in Scotland. Prince Albert officially opened it and, on 18th June, Queen Victoria made a special visit. In her honour a Highland gathering and a balloon ascent by Captain Dale was held. Great prestige was brought to the city by the exhibition and to this day you can still see a few remains of this international event.

93. Considered by many as one of the finest concert halls in Europe, Usher Hall was the generous gift of Edinburgh brewer Andrew Usher. The foundation stone was laid by King George V and Queen Mary on 19th July 1911 and the building was officially opened three years later. During the world-famous Edinburgh International Festival, held in late August each year, this magnificent concert hall hosts some of the finest orchestras, conductors and artists from all over the world.

94. The interior of Usher Hall is as beautiful as the exterior. It has a seating capacity of 3,500 for concerts and seats are at a premium when the greatest orchestras and artists come to Edinburgh. During the Edinburgh International Festival each August, when people come from all over the world, these seats are filled to capacity. At the present time the great organ is silent, but plans have been made for its complete restoration and the American Organist Carlo Curley is said to be the organist who will play the first concert after its restoration.

A Fruit and Grain Corner in Edinburgh
(Tarvit Street and Leven Street).

J. R. R. E.

95. There is much activity at the 'Fruit and Grain Corner' at Leven and Tarvit Streets. The corner shop is a branch of Covent Garden, Leith and has strawberries and gooseberries for sale. A horse-drawn cart is loading or unloading as pedestrians stroll by in more leisurely days at the turn of the century. The tall chimney behind the shops is that of the Drumdryan Brewery, established in 1760. One of the reasons that Edinburgh can boast of so many fine breweries, is because of its very fine water, that to the present time has produced world class beers and ales. All of these buildings disappeared when the King's Theatre was built on the site and opened in 1906.

The Causewayside Edinburgh, in 1850 — looking South.

96. Causewayside Toll, as seen in this postcard, had disappeared. Today it is a busy part of the city, just a few hundred yards from the Meadows. Early last century Causewayside Toll and Dalkeith Road, nearby, were the two main roads into the capital city from the south. At one time this area was called 'The village of Sciennes', where handloom weaving flourished in nearby Grange Court. From 1850 onward, however, the area grew rapidly and soon became overcrowded and unruly. Barriers, like those in this photograph, were set up at Salisbury Place and Duncan Street to 'protect' the wealthy residents in the large and fashionable houses between Minto Street and Dalkeith Road from the rowdy people of Causewayside Toll.

The "Innocent Railway" Station, the oldest in Scotland, St. Leonard's Lane Edinburgh,
(near Jeanie Deans' Cottage.) (1826—1842).
J. R. R. — E.

97. This rare postcard shows the 'Innocent Railway' Station, opened in July 1831 at St. Leonard's Lane. This was the first station in Edinburgh, not in Scotland, as the postcard states. It linked together a number of collieries including those in Millerhill, Niddrie, and the Woolmet Pit. From St. Leonard's the railway ran to Newtongrange and Dalkeith with branches to Fisherrow and Leith. The station was reached by a single line from Duddingston through Holyrood Park past Arthur's Seat and through a tunnel at the Wells o'Wearie. At first only coal was carried, but it soon became a tourist attraction and permission was granted to carry passengers in 1843. On holidays as many as 20,000 passengers were carried each day and 300,000 each year. The wooden carriages were pulled by horses until 1845, when steam locomotives replaced them. By 1870 passengers were no longer using this service, for they preferred the newer Waverley and suburban line stations. The railway was called 'Innocent' because it never had a fatal accident in its entire lifetime.

SALISBURY CRAGS, EDINBURGH.

Courtesy L. M. S. R.

35

98. There is no city in the world that has such a fascinating geological formation in a park in the middle of town as Edinburgh. It is called Salisbury Crags in Queens Park and is seen in this postcard above what is known as the Radical Road. Millions of years ago it was formed from the once active volcano called Arthur's Seat. Geologists have found Salisbury Crags one of the most interesting spots in Britain. The people of Edinburgh are proud of their city and its beautiful parks and they have every right to be, because there is no other city that can claim such a spectacular and unique sight. Salisbury Crags is over 450 feet above sea level and can be seen from vantage points all over the city.

The Peak Arthur's Seat, Edinburgh.

99. Arthur's Seat is an extinct volcano but still fascinates as it dominates the skyline of 'Auld Reekie'. It stands 829 feet above sea level and from its summit, on a clear day the gateway to the Highlands 40 miles away can be seen. Spectacular views can also be seen of the Firth of Forth valley, the Kingdom of Fife, the city itself and the hills that surround Edinburgh to the south. This postcard shows a group that has made the ascent for the views and refreshments. The young boy serves as assistance to the older man standing for the photograph in his white apron. He is the lemonade vendor offering a bottle to the boy who is opening his picnic hamper. The tablecloth spread on the rocks displays the stock of the lemonade vendor. Volumes have been written about Arthur's Seat. Boswell said of her long ago: 'It is no common crest but, given the proper day and suitable illumination from a broken sky, the natural shrine of a folk-memory of the heroic sort. And under it, when the clouds come low, the smoke of the encroaching houses will dance a witches' dance and ''Auld Reekie'' can be seen in all her wicked past.'

100. Curling began in Scotland in the 16th century and was played by the elite of Edinburgh on the Nor' Loch in what is now Princes Street Gardens. The Duddingston Curling Society is said to be the oldest in the world, formed in 1795. They have every right to make this claim because they established, in 1803, the first rules of the game that are the basis for the rules by which the game is played to this day throughout the world. This rare early picture, taken from a stereoscopic view of last century, shows the members of Duddingston Club curling on their loch with the Duddingston Church of Scotland, a Norman kirk, in the background. In the garden of the Manse, Sir Walter Scott, an elder of Duddingston Kirk, while visiting his Minister, Reverend John Thomson, wrote some of the chapters of 'The Heart of Midlothian'.

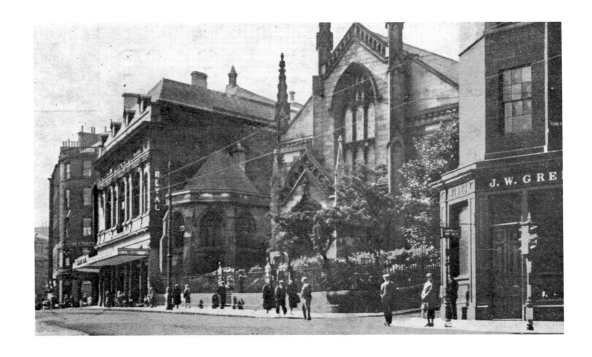

101. The Theatre Royal, built in 1884 to replace the Theatre of the same name where the General Post Office now stands, is seen on the left of St. Mary's Roman Catholic Cathedral, and occupies a site that, since 1853, has been home to four theatres that have burnt down. Pictured here is one of these homes. In March 1946 this building was destroyed by fire and the Theatre Royal is now only a happy memory for many of the people of Edinburgh. This entire site, with the exception of the Cathedral, is now occupied by the huge St. James' Centre, a modern shopping mall. Gone are the days of vaudeville when the citizens of the city were entertained by top class artists at the Royal and the dozen or so other theatres scattered throughout the city. Today television has changed the habits of people to such an extent that theatres and cinemas have had to struggle to stay alive.

102. This is the house and law office of Sir Walter Scott at 39 Castle Street. He was the son of a solicitor born at 39 College Wynd in the Old Town in 1771. At the age of 18 months he contracted polio that left him with a permanent limp to his right leg. Scott distinguished himself as a great writer and respected advocate, who was appointed Clerk of the Court of Session in 1806, a position he held until 1830. It was as an author of romantic narrative poems, such as 'Marmion' and 'The Lady of the Lake', as well as his historical novels that Sir Walter Scott won world-wide fame for himself and created international interest in Scotland. This international interest that he began through his writing has continued to this day. He was an honourable man, who became involved in an unfortunate financial crisis with his publisher, Ballantynes of Edinburgh, and became a debtor. He spent the rest of his life at his beloved country home at Abbotsford, on the River Tweed near Melrose, where he wrote his famous 'Waverley Novels'. Although ill and weary, he succeeded in paying back everything he owed before his death in 1832. This in itself was a heroic act.

103. At the west end of Melville Street stands what many believe to be one of the most beautiful churches built in Scotland since the Reformation, St. Mary's Scottish Episcopal Cathedral. It was begun in 1874 to the design of Sir Gilbert Scott and finished five years later. From the earliest days of St. Mary's, an outstanding music school, originally called the 'Sang School', has been associated with the work of the Cathedral and admired and appreciated by the citizens of Edinburgh. Many of its gifted pupils have gone on to bring honour to their Cathedral Music School and to distinguish themselves as musicians.

Edinburgh   *English Cathedral*

104. James Donaldson, proprietor of the long defunct newspaper 'The Edinburgh Advertiser', bequeathed most of his estate, when he died in 1830, for the care of poor boys and girls. This picture postcard shows the palatial Donaldson's Hospital, built in Tudor style in 1850. It was designed by the famous Edinburgh architect Playfair. The school accommodated 218 children, half of whom were deaf and dumb. It is often said that Queen Victoria admired this building so much that she would have preferred this to be the Palace rather than Holyrood House, that had a brewery nearby. The smell of beer brewing annoyed the 'tea-totler' Queen.

The Orphan's Hospital, Edinburgh

105. The magnificent Orphan's Hospital seen in this postcard is located in the Dean part of the city off Queensferry Road. Although the orphans who lived here were poor, they had a handsome building in which to live and it still stands today, without exterior alterations, as it did in 1883, when it was built to a design by Thomas Hamilton. Most of the 120 boys and girls who lived here were admitted free, but a few paid an annual board of between £14 and £16. The interior of the building was spartan, with dark brown walls to hide the finger marks of children. In the basement was a bare room with a grey rocking horse. Every year there was an open day with a picnic on the grounds for the children, their friends, and their relations. Today this beautiful building is used as a training college for nurses. Notice the sheep grazing, even in the middle of a capital city, on the lawn in front of the building. This was very common, before modern machinery. Throughout the green areas of the city these peaceful animals kept the lawns well-trimmed while at the same time they fed themselves. This was a practical solution to a difficult problem.

Dean Bridge, Edinburgh

Printed by V. & S., Ltd., D., for the Picture Post Card Bureau, Edinburgh.

106. Thomas Telford's beautiful bridge over the Dean Village and Water of Leith was opened in 1832. Even to this day it carries most of the city's traffic to and from Queensferry and the north. From humble origins, the son of a border shepherd, Telford, distinguished himself by his majestic bridges, none more beautiful than the Dean, and deserved the title he was given in his time: 'The Colossus of Roads.' Dean Village, once known as Water of Leith Village, is one of Edinburgh's most picturesque villages. It was once the home of mills powered by the Water of Leith. Today these disused mills have been made into attractive flats and this unique village, in the middle of a busy capital city, has become an oasis of quiet and calm.

ALEX. FERGUSON'S SWEET-MEAT FACTORY
STAND 294, Machinery Hall, Scottish National Exhibition, Edinburgh 1908

107. The Scottish National Exhibition was held in 1908 in Saughton, where North British Railway built a special station on the main line to bring passengers from the centre of the city to the site. The aim of this exhibition was to exemplify all that was best in art, science, industry and literature in Scotland and many of the exhibits seemed to accomplish that aim. This rare postcard shows the interior of Alex Ferguson's unusual kiosk. The upper part of his building was a replica of Edinburgh City's coat of arms, and the lower part a rock temple that was called 'Edinburgh Rock.' Alex Ferguson was, for many years, the manufacturer of the famous confection called 'Edinburgh Rock' and was a favourite present purchased by visitors for friends and relatives back home.

R. L STEVENSON FROM BUST IN NATIONAL PORTRAIT
GALLERY.

108. Of all the literature from the world famous authors of Edinburgh none is more loved than the writings of Robert Louis Stevenson. His books 'Kidnapped' and 'Dr. Jekyll and Mr. Hyde' have been made into movies and they are read by adults and children in all the major languages of the world. Stevenson was born in the New Town and lived there as a boy at Heriot Row. He is the son of a famous family of lighthouse engineers and as a young student at University, where he was known for his rebellious nature and colourful lifestyle, began his studies in engineering and then changed to the faculty of law and became an advocate. As a child he was often ill and the damp climate and smoke-filled air of 'Auld Reekie', with whom he had a love-hate relationship, finally forced him to move to a more suitable climate. During his travels he met and married the American Fanny Osbourne, whose influence upon the rest of his life brought him great happiness. They settled in Samoa, where he built his home, farmed the land and wrote until his death in 1894. He would smile with pleasure, no doubt, if he knew that there stands in the National Portrait Gallery on Queen Street, not very far from where he spent his happy boyhood days in his beloved city, a bust of himself.